THE MYTH & MAGIC OF CATS

BY ARIANNA REYNOLDS

QUARTERLY

yearBOOKS,INC.
Dr. Herbert R. Axelrod,
Founder & Chairman

Dominique De Vito
Chief Editor

yearBOOKS are all photo composed, color separated and designed on Scitex equipment in Neptune, N.J. with the following staff:

DIGITAL PRE-PRESS
Patricia Northrup
Supervisor

Robert Onyrscuk
Jose Reyes

COMPUTER ART
Patti Escabi
Sandra Taylor Gale
Candida Moreira
Joanne Muzyka
Francine Shulman

ADVERTISING SALES
Nancy S. Rivadeneira
Advertising Sales Director
Cheryl J. Blyth
Advertising Account Manager
Amy Manning
Advertising Director
Sandy Cutillo
Advertising Coordinator

©yearBOOKS, Inc.
1 TFH Plaza
Neptune, N.J. 07753
Completely manufactured in
Neptune, N.J.
USA

Exploring the origin of the domestic cat uncovers a fascinating and mysterious history.

WHAT ARE QUARTERLIES?

Books, the usual way information of this sort is transmitted, can be too slow. Sometimes by the time a book is written and published, the material contained therein is a year or two old...and no new material has been added during that time. Only a book in a magazine form can bring breaking stories and current information. A magazine is streamlined in production, so we have adopted certain magazine publishing techniques in the creation of this Cat Quarterly. Magazines also can be much less expensive than books because they are supported by advertising. To combine these assets into a great publication, we issued this Quarterly in both magazine and book format at different prices.

Contents

Photography by Isabelle Francais, Robert Pearcy.

The Origin of Domestic Cats

The cat, full of primeval ferocity, mystery and unpredictability, is a creature that has fascinated humans from the beginning of time. Why is this so, and what qualities does this animal have that have made it the focus of both worship and persecution? The cat is all we love and fear embodied in a single form. It is a creature of indisputed beauty, both in its appearance and in its movements. It is a creature of great patience, a virtue we all admire, yet its unbridled ferocity gives us good reason to treat it with respect. Indeed, in the form of the lion or leopard, it is one of the most feared of all predators.

The cat is a creature of great strength, agility and speed, abilitlies we struggle to achieve in ourselves. Yet at night, those glowing eyes that stare into your very soul have given rise to the belief that here was a demonic being in animal form. To understand how we have come to regard the domestic cat, we must wander through the ages and across continents, in order to start the story from the very beginning.

The cat's background hosts a long lineage that includes such notables as the leopard.

The cat represents the magnificent combination of graceful agility and powerful strength.

FELINE EVOLUTION

Long before the great dinosaurs died out at the end of the Cretaceous period, 65 million years ago, the earliest ancestors of the cat were beginning to evolve. This was 200 million years ago, when the Theriodonts, or mammal-toothed reptiles, were roaming the earth. These warm-blooded reptiles were a far cry from a cat, looking more like long-legged crocodiles with shortened jaws. They gave rise to the dog-jawed reptiles, such as those of the genus *Cynognathus*. These creatures probably had fur, so the beginning of true mammals was underway.

By the Eocene epoch, 54-38 million years ago, a group of animals known as the miacids had developed. These were small (maybe two feet in length), slim-bodied, tree-climbing carnivores that were the "improved" creodonts. Their senses—especially those of smell, sight and hearing—were highly developed. Their strength and agility distinguished them from the more primitive meat-eaters that would eventually die out.

From the miacids evolved the dinictids (*Dinictis*), which were the first of the groups that can be regarded as true cats. They lived 38-7 million years ago. Among these were both the biting and the stabbing cats. The stabbing cats are better known as the saber-toothed cats. It is from the false saber-tooths that all present day felids developed during the last two million years. These dinictids were about the size of the lynx, but had longer fangs—and maybe smaller brains. So the cat was to grow wiser the longer it stayed on our planet!

During the last great Ice Age, which ended only 20,000 years ago, the ice-land bridges caused the sort of cataclysm that created the downfall of the dinosaurs. Migration of species from one continent to the other resulted in many species from the saber-toothed cats to the woolly mammoths to disappear forever. In their wake, new species, both grazing and predatory, found they could prosper. Among these were the roaring cats—modern lions, leopards and jaguars—all of which represent the youngest branch of the felid line.

THE DOMESTICATION OF CATS

While each of our present-day cat species was steadily evolving, there were other creatures that were doing the same, these being the primates. One of these was eventually to become Homo sapiens, better known as humans. So when and where did the paths of humans and cats meet and come together? The answer to this may never be known because it may well have happened before humans knew how to write. All that can be done is to search for clues that might indicate the reason people wanted to share their homes with a cat.

In Egypt

While the first great civilization, that of the Egyptians, may or may not have been responsible for domesticating the cat, it cannot be denied that it was the people of the Nile delta who were responsible for creating the human concept of the cat in relation to its characteristics—both real and believed. These concepts were to shape the way that all civilizations would view these magnificent creatures.

From Egyptian artifacts, it can be said that the cat was certainly domesticated by about 1500 B.C.—probably even earlier.

It is also probable that the cat aroused the interest of the early Egyptians because they saw it kill mice and rats, and these rodents stole much of the stored grain. It would have been useful to encourage the cat to live in the vicinity of the grain stores, and, from there, in people's homes.

This came to pass, and the Egyptians began to idolize their new friend. They saw most things around them as being the agents of good or evil, and the cat was perceived as representing those things that were good. The cat came to be regarded as the earthly image of their gods. They did not believe it was a god in itself, only that it was one of many forms in which their sun and moon gods could come to earth. The pharaoh himself was the actual god on earth, all others being best regarded as his assistants.

Although the cat gods and goddesses were often worshipped in the form of lions, or lionheaded humans, many of these came to be replaced by the cat, as the cult of the cat grew in popularity. After all, you could not keep a lion in your home, but you could keep a small cat. The cat goddess was called Bast, or Bastet, and her home was in the city of Bubastis in the Nile delta. She was a cat-headed woman and, with the passage of time, became one of the most important of the Egyptian gods.

Bast was associated with fertility, happiness, music, and many other characteristics that endeared her to her followers. In the great temples, real cats were kept, and their welfare

The Egyptians are credited with initially domesticating the cat; represented here is the stately Egyptian Mau.

The cat goddess Bast was worshipped in Egyptian civilization, and often depicted in the art of the period.

became the responsibility of honored priests, whose position was inhereted. They waited for "signs" from the cats, and tried to interpret their every action.

The death penalty existed in Egypt for any person who killed a cat deliberately. If it was an accident, then a large fine was levied. If the cat died a natural death, it was a time for great mourning. People shaved their eyebrows, and the cat was mummified and buried with solemn ritual. Wealthier people encased their cherished pets in a miniature sarcophagus and even mummified mice so the cat would have food on its journey to the hereafter.

Many cats were taken each year to the great cat festival at Bubastis, where they were buried in communal graves (as they were in numerous other areas by people who could not afford the journey to this city). In one grave, no less than 300,000 mummies were preserved. In 1907, the British Museum obtained 192 cat mummies dating from 600-200 B.C..

The cat was so highly revered in Egyptian culture that many were mummified to ensure the journey to the Afterlife.

In Europe

Although Egypt forbade the export of cats, it is obvious that as long as there was a market for them in certain lands, ways would be found to obtain them. In Greece, as in Rome, rodents were a problem. These people tried to use polecats to control the mice and rats, but this proved futile. Tamed snakes were also unsuccessful. The cat alone was the answer, so a healthy smuggling trade was established.

It is probable that cats had become established in Greece and the islands of the Aegean well before Greece ever became a united country. The same applies to Italy and the land of the Romans. North Africa, the civilization based at Carthage found practical advantage in having cats in the vicinity of both docks and granaries. However, in all of these countries, while the cat was revered for its ability to control rodent populations, it never reached the level of being worshipped the way it was in Egypt.

The spread of the cat into Europe must be credited to the Romans, whose legions campaigned in Spain, France, Germany, and ultimately, Britain. In the United Kingdom, the first domestic cats may have arrived during the First Century B.C.. It is possible that the Phoenicians, who pioneered the Atlantic, may also have been involved in bringing the cat to Britain, via Ireland.

At first, it was thought that cats were only kept by wealthy Romans. This changed once many of the legions were recalled to defend the Roman Empire in

In Greece and Rome, the value of a cat was determined by a more practical criterion—the ability to control rodents.

Germany and Gaul (France). Many cats became feral and, as forests steadily gave way to fields, these cats probably supplanted the more wild cats found in Britain and throughout Europe. The domestic cat's value becomes apparent when we learn of some laws enacted by Howell the Good, a Prince of South Wales in 936 A.D.. A kitten was worth one penny (a great deal of money in those days), but as it grew and proved its ability to catch mice, its value grew as well. An adult mouser was worth about four pence.

Cats were quite commonplace in the monasteries of Europe, where they continued their role as mousers. However, they were also used as a source of fur. In 1127, a decree was issued that any furs worn by people must reflect their social status. Monks, for example, were not allowed to wear a fur that was more costly than that of either a sheep or a cat.

Cats have been voyagers in epic charters around the globe.

Because cats proved invaluable in controlling rodent populations aboard sailing ships, they were transported, free of charge, to exotic ports of call.

In America

The cat arrived in the New World via the early emigrants from England, Spain, and other nations. However, the cat may well have been in America by the time Columbus discovered the New World during the 15th century. It is possible that the Vikings may have introduced it some centuries earlier. Could the cats from the Norsemen live on as the Maine Coon breed? They closely resembled the cat known as the Norwegian Forest cat in Scandinavia.

There are two reasons cats were taken around the world by explorers: The first was that they helped to eradicate the rodents that always managed to get onto the ships and destroy food supplies, and cargo; the second was that once the ships landed and settlements were established, the cat continued its role as the protector of grain and other foods.

Through human transportation, the cat has been taken to every country and to most of the world's islands. It is such an adaptable creature that with or without human help, it is able to rapidly multiply and survive. On some subarctic islands, feral cat populations have prospered even after they have decimated the rodents. Cats have skill to catch fish and marine invertebrates, as well as sea birds. The domestic and feral cat is now the most successful cat species to ever walk our planet.

Due to its ability to adapt to a variety of environments and circumstances, the cat is often considered the most adaptable species on the planet.

The feline's mesmerizing stare plays a pivotal role in its association with the occult.

Cat Myths And Fables

The cat has been the subject of myths and fables since it first became domesticated. There is almost no country that does not have stories that either praise or vilify the qualities thought to be inherent in all cats. We can only mention a few of these here, but they fully illustrate the fact that the cat has had a very powerful impact on the different people of the world.

In most instances, the godly image of the cat in Egypt was transported—to a greater or lesser degree—to all parts of the world. It was then integrated into the beliefs of other nations. In the process, new features were attributed to it, and new stories were told of both its domestication and its powers.

In Arizona, there is a legend told by the Hopi Indians of how the cat came to be domesticated. A little boy found a strange animal under a rock and took it home. His father recognized that it was a cat, which fed on rabbits and rodents. The boy locked the cat up and went hunting for rabbits, which he fed to the cat until it was tame. Since that time, the cat has lived with the Hopi and kept their homes free of mice and rats.

Another tale of domestication comes from Asia. It is said that the tiger lived with the cat, and when one day the tiger became feverish, the cat searched for fire to warm his friend. But only man possessed fire, so the cat entered man's home. There he saw rice and fish near the hearth, and it was beyond his power to refuse such a feast, so he ate it and fell asleep on the hearth. When he awoke, he remembered his friend, so he took a burning fire stick to give him warmth. He then told the tiger that he had found a better life, and would

The rabbit and the cat feature prominently in a fable popularized by Hopi Indians.

thereafter leave the jungle to live in the home of man, who had good food and the warmth of a fire.

Then there is the story of how the cat got into Noah's Ark. It would seem that the cat and the pig were not among the animals taken into the Ark because God had not created them. Because the pig was absent, sewage began to accumulate, becoming a threat to those who sheltered inside. With no cats around, rats and mice were breeding and nibbling the walls of the Ark, presenting a real danger. Noah patted the elephant on its back, and a pig jumped from its trunk and ate the sewage. Noah then patted the lion on the forehead, and a cat jumped from its nose. The cat put things in order among the mice and rats so that they would not nibble at the walls of the Ark.

An old Chinese fable tells of Pe, who owned pigeons. Pe noticed that a cat had stolen some of his pigeons, so he caught it and cut off his feet. Nine more cats were doomed to a similar fate, but the heavens punished the villain.

Even Noah purportedly appreciated the cat's contribution to keeping the Ark afloat!

Many cultures and religions include the cat in their legends and popular folklore.

His wife gave birth to nine children, and all were born without either arms or legs.

There is also an old Chinese legend that tells of a doctor who replaced the diseased eye of a peasant with that of a cat. The operation was a success, and the peasant could see with the cat's eye as if it were his own. Unfortunately, he could not close the cat's eye at night, because he felt the irresistible urge to seek out rats!

There are numerous stories that have been handed down that relate to Buddha. One tells that when Buddha was dying, all of the animals gathered around his deathbed in lament. The rat was there and began to lick the oil from the lamp near the bed. On seeing this, the cat killed the rat and ate it. This seemingly natural act was regarded as a sin, for Buddha had proclaimed love between all living creatures. In another version of this story, the cat killed the rat, which was bringing medicine to the dying Buddha, so the cat alone amidst all the animals, was not allowed to attend the funeral of this great man.

In Japan, the beckoning cat is a symbol of good luck and prosperity. Such cats are seen in front of stores, temples, and restaurants, and you can purchase cat amulets in the form of good luck charms in stores. But how did this association come about? It is told that many years ago, there was a very poor temple that was made of nothing but mud bricks. In it lived equally poor priests whose spiritual leader owned a cat. One day, six Samurai warriors were

Buddhists established the beckoning cat as a symbol of good fortune and prosperity.

riding by when they noticed the cat sitting with one of its paws raised to its ear as though beckoning them. They dismounted, and as the cat continued to beckon, they followed it into the temple. A raging thunderstorm then followed, so the Samurais stayed awhile and listened to the priests tell stories of Buddha.

One of the warriors, a Lord Li, returned many times to the little temple to receive instruction on the doctrines of the Buddha. As time passed, he endowed the temple with lands and riches, and it became the home of his family. Today, when visitors pass through the impressive archways and gardens of the Gotoku-ji temple, they can see the cemetery of the Li family. Near this, they can also see the small shrine of the cat that, to this day, still beckons people to visit this temple in Tokyo.

The proud stance of cats like this Oriental Shorthair inspired a noble image in certain tales and legends.

But the cat was not always favored in Japan and other countries. Even when it was considered a good omen, this did not always work in its favor. In China and other Far Eastern countries, for example, the eye of the cat was thought to ward off evil demons. As a result, the poor house cat was chained up near a door to prevent the demons from entering. In many other countries, having the real cat was preferred, but it was also thought that an image of the cat was equally effective. It is for this reason that you will often see cat figurines and paintings above or alongside the doors of many Far Eastern homes and businesses. Some of these are extremely ferocious or demonic looking. This is because the Chinese felt that the uglier the cat, the more effective it was in frightening away the demons of the night.

From its earliest days with humans, the cat has always been associated with fertility, and with feminine traits. As a result, in most cultures you will find it has often been regarded as both a good and bad omen in respect to females and their ability to bear children. For many people, a cat seen near an altar during a marriage ceremony was a bad omen for the couple. Yet in another culture, it could be a good one. Newlyweds in Thailand are considered very lucky if they are given a pair of Korat cats, while in England a black cat model is often placed in a horseshoe, both being signs of good luck.

While in many cultures a black cat is seen as a sign of good luck, in others it is thought to foretell misfortune. Likewise, a white cat may be indicative of good or bad luck, depending not only in which country one lives, but even which part of that country one lives. Even among African tribes are found many fables and stories surrounding the cat. Whatever the culture and wherever the country, it is sure to have stories of this night stalker, whose enigmatic shining eyes create an aura of mystery.

Throughout history, black and white cats have been associated with both good *and* bad luck, depending on the source of the fable.

The hypnotic effect of a cat's eyes has inspired many popular narratives.

It may be difficult for cat lovers to imagine their beloved creatures as victims of such heinous behavior in centuries past.

THE ERA OF PERSECUTION

The benevolence that had been accorded the cat for centuries, began to change in Medieval Europe and England as a result of Christianity. The cat, which had for so many centuries enjoyed a favored standing with humans, could now only dream about the peaceful life of its ancestors. Just reading about the horrors perpetuated on felines

The eradication of cats contributed to the spread of plagues throughout Europe, due to the vast increase in rodent populations. Ironically, this served to reaffirm the cat's value to humankind.

is hard, but they illustrate what an indifferent and cruel species humans can be.

In the 15th century, ministers of the Christian faith held witch hunts and persecuted many animals, the cat in particular. Black cats suffered even worse than those of other colors. Supernatural forces were attributed to cats and witches. They were thought to be able to do magic, cast spells on people and enter their homes to take over their souls in the dead of the night. Cats were thought to be able

The cat's natural agility proved to be one of its few available defenses in escaping persecution.

to turn into witches and demons, and to be able to fly. When cats congregated, this was a sure indication that, come nighttime, they would hold satanic rituals.

As a result of these feline deprivations, cats were burnt, beaten, stoned to death, hanged, quartered, thrown onto rubbish heaps with their paws cut off, and blinded. They were buried alive, boiled in oil, and thrown from church belfries. With the population of cats being so drastically reduced, rats

began to breed on an enormous scale and created many plagues, such as the great plague of London, the Black Death, which spread and killed millions of people.

You would think this would have brought sanity to the people of this time, but the poor cat was even blamed for this, and every other human misfortune. People's hatred of cats turned into a cult of killing them by every means possible. In Denmark, there was a tradition of placing the

Few cats were spared the stigma of degradation in pagan times.

cat in a barrel and hanging the barrel from a tree. Horsemen would spear the barrel, the winner being the one who broke the barrel and killed the cat. In England, the cat was placed in a leather bag and used as a target by archers. The old saying of "letting the cat out of the bag" derives from these practices.

A cat's focal vision is equal to that of a human; however, felines have far superior lateral vision.

In Spain, there existed a cat organ, which when its keys were pressed, pulled on the cat's tail. A hammer then hit the cat's tail causing the poor wretch to mew desperately. In 1344 in Metz, France, an epidemic broke out, and the devil in the form of a cat was held to be the guilty party. Thirteen cats were placed into a cage and burned alive, and this became an annual ritual.

Another ritual that was practiced for centuries throughout Europe, was that of entombing a live cat in the walls of a building, or its foundations. This was thought to protect the house from mice, rats, and demons. In Germany, as in other countries, an especially horrific rite was to bury a cat or dog alive in a plowed field. This was thought to prevent thistles from growing! In western Pomerania, a cat or dog was buried alive under a fruit tree in order that it would bear fruit. In Finland, it was thought that the more cats that were buried in fields, the greater would be the harvest. These various notions about burying a cat no doubt came from the believed descriptions of Sabbats - the meetings of the Devil, sometimes in the form of a black cat, and his followers.

At such gatherings, the disciples would file past the devil and kiss his posterior. They would make offerings of unbaptized children and reaffirm their vows to the devil. A feast would follow, after which they would tell of their deeds since the last meeting. The most favored witches would be those who had caused the most disease among people and their cattle, and who had spoilt the most fruit and grain. The more spells they had placed, the greater their standing in the coven of witches. After this, there would be drinking and dancing, which would lead to sexual orgies that were continued until dawn.

This constant association of the cat with the Devil, and

Even a creature as innocent as this small kitten was caught in the tide of malevolence during pagan times.

The cat's natural beauty was shrouded in dark mystery in centuries past.

with sexuality, is not difficult to understand. You must remember that we are talking, for the most part, about ignorant peasant people. Consider the female cat when she is in heat. It has to be agreed that she is obviously in a highly sexual state. In the prone position, with her posterior held upwards, this is very suggestive of a wanton animal. The wailings of both feline sexes at night, coupled with the fighting of the toms for the favor of the queens, was easily misunderstood to be the goings-on of the Devil in simple people's minds. The night shine of the cat's eyes can make even present day folk nervous in the right setting, so you can imagine what it did to the peasants of

An ancient association with cats lives on today in our celebration of Halloween.

a few centuries ago. The cat's habit of sniffing the anal region of its fellows gave proof to the peasants that Devil worship was true.

The ferocity of a cornered cat with its claws outstretched, its fur on end, back arched, and its bared fangs when it hissed, were all seen as indications of its demonic associations. The fact that the cat is so independent certainly did not help its cause. This persecution of cats lasted until well into the 19th century, although by this time things had generally improved for felines over the previous 100 years.

It should not be thought that cat persecution was a purely European phenomenon, because it was also seen in Eastern and Far Eastern countries, though on a much smaller scale. In Turkey, one way of punishing an unfaithful wife was to place her in a sack, hands tied, with two or three cats, then drop her into a river. The

frenzied cats would rip away at the poor woman's body. Sometimes all were left to drown; sometimes they would be released on the assumption that the female would think twice before again being unfaithful to her husband. Here, the cat was the tool, rather than the object, of the torture. In Japan, it was a common belief that cats could turn into vampires, a result of which many were killed.

In order to place some perspective on the situation, it should be mentioned that cats were not alone in being associated with the Devil. The dog, but more so the goat, also paid the price of having had earlier pagan associations. They, too, were tried and tortured along with their witch owners.

Strange as it may seem, not all cats were persecuted, so we find that both nobility and ordinary folk, rich and poor, also adored cats during these dark centuries. Even members of the clergy, while

It is a tribute to felines' innate resilience that they survived this horrific period of history.

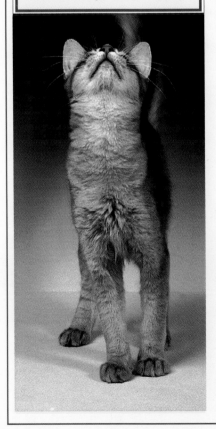

fanning the flames of witch hunts and feline torture, were known to keep cats. It would seem that much depended on who owned the cats in determining whether they were demons in disguise. In some countrysides, a cat was left alone as long as it did not enter a home, which indicated it was seeking to weave a spell on the inhabitants.

Official persecution of the cat seems to have stopped by the beginning of the 18th century, at which time people were starting to question some of the religious doctrines. However, old habits die hard, and in the more rural areas of a country, the legends and myths that surrounded the cat were not easily put aside. As a result, the cat continued to be the subject of cruelty until well into the 19th century.

Because people could not accept the cat for what it really was, there was a need to try to explain its character in wholly unnatural terms. The many religious sects that sprang up after the fall of Rome were themselves regarded as pagan and heretical by the orthodox religions. These sought to vilify anything that had a connection with past beliefs. As the cat was high on the list of those which had been worshiped as almost divine, it was essential that these be the subject of special degradation. The term "Dark Ages" was not only applicable to an unfortunate period in human history, but was especially so for our feline friends.

It was this black period in the cat's history that

prompted Harrison Weir, the Father of the Cat Fancy, to draw our attention to the beauty of cats when he organized the world's first cat show in 1871. As he stated, "The shadow of cruelty lying on a miserable cat's existence will disappear in the course of only several generations." This has come to pass, and the cat is once again regarded in high esteem—at least in the more advanced countries of the world. Not only have the people of most nations adopted the cat as their favorite pet, but you can again see these creatures of the night silently treading the hallowed courtyards and corridors of churches. Even their most hostile persecutors came to realize that in the cat they had not an enemy to be feared, but a friend to be treated with kindness.

It is certainly easy to see how the cat population could have diminished significantly considering the torment endured by cats centuries ago.

Black cats were routinely sacrificed in demonic rituals during the Dark Ages.

The late nineteenth century brought a period of enlightenment, and a renewed appreciation of the cat.

Famous People & Famous Cats

Over the centuries, there have been many famous people who have shown a special love for their pets, be they horses, dogs, birds, or, for our interest, cats. It is always interesting to read about these people, both those who were real, and those who were created in literature and drawings.

You have just read how terribly cats were treated during the last few centuries, so it is nice to know that at least some members of the clergy adored their cats. Cardinal Richelieu, the French statesman (1585-1642), left a large sum of money so that the 14 cats he owned would be well cared for after he died. Interestingly, one of his cats was called Lucifer!

Pope Leo XII (1760-1829), was another man of the cloth who was a great cat lover. One of his favorites, called Micetta, was actually born in the Vatican. The English Cardinal Thomas Wolsey lived at a time (16th century) when cats were considered to be on the wrong side of the church, yet his favored feline used to attend mass with him!

In another religion, the great prophet Mohammed (570-632) of the Muslim faith, owned a cat called Meuzza. One day, he was asleep on the sleeve of his robe when the prophet was called to prayer. Mohammed cut off his sleeve so his pet would not be disturbed. Legend has it that it was Mohammed who granted the cat the ability to always land on his feet when falling from a height. He also ensured that in the Muslim faith, cats would be well thought of.

The famed Nobel peace prize winner Dr. Albert

Because of its luxurious coat and sensual appearance, the Persian cat is often featured as the pampered feline in television commercials.

Even the great English "Bulldog," Winston Churchill, enjoyed the company of felines.

Schweitzer (1875-1965) loved all animals, but had a soft spot for his cat, Suzy. Albert was left-handed, but would often change the pen to his other hand in order not to disturb Suzy, who had the habit of sleeping on his arm. Of course, this attitude is known to all cat lovers: don't we always sleep in the most uncomfortable of configurations so as not to disturb our sleeping feline friends!

One of the world's great leaders, Winston Churchill, the British Prime Minister of World War II fame, was an ardent cat lover. He had many cats, but during the war, his cat Nelson (named for another great English hero), had its own place in the Cabinet room, and at the dining table. On his 88th birthday, Churchill was given a cat called Jock, which became very well known at the statesman's Chartwell home. Winston would often insist that he could not eat his dinner until the cat was there also. He left a sum of money so that there should be a "marmalade" cat in his Chartwell home forever. This money, he said, was to cover "board and lodging."

The famous English writer Samuel Johnson (1709-84) was yet another famous person "owned" by a cat, whose name was Hodge. Johnson always shopped for oysters for Hodge himself so that the servants would not feel hostile for having to wait on the cat. Other famous authors who owned cats include Charles Dickens and Alexandre Dumas. One author who really loved cats was Ernest Hemingway. He

Cats can indeed be trained and so their talents are often utilized in feature films and on television.

kept about thirty in his Havana, Cuba, home. This, however, is only half the number owned by the famous nurse Florence Nightingale (1820-1910).

The English writer Edward Lear who, apart from producing some superb paintings of birds for the Zoological Society of London, also wrote that whimsical story, *The Owl and The Pussy Cat*, was truly a cat lover. When he left England to live in Italy, he had a house built

Families of five toed cats have inhabited Ernest Hemingway's estate in Key West since the author himself was in residence.

that was an exact replica of his former home so that his cat Floss would not be upset over the move.

American president Calvin Coolidge (1872-1933) owned both a cat, Timmie, and a canary. The canary became a great friend of the cat and would hop up and down its back, singing happily. Not all presidents, however, can be enumerated as cat lovers, for Dwight Eisenhower (1890-1960) hated them so much that he ordered them to be shot if they appeared near his house. Another great general, Napoleon Bonaparte (1769-1821), also hated cats, and would break out in a rage and a sweat if one got near to him. The American lexicographer, Noah Webster (1758-1843), was another famous person who had little good to say about cats—which only goes to show that even some of the great people down through the ages had some major flaws in their character!

Appointing himself the Emperor of France was a real feather in his cap, but the sight of this cat with a feather would have absolutely petrified Napoleon!

Many cat owners place their cats on a royal pedestal, much like this Himalayan kitten.

SOME FAMOUS CATS

Cats have been the subject of both many poems and fairy tales, and real cats have become very famous as a result of their promotional use, selling cat foods and other products. One of the best known was called Morris, a ginger tom. He died in 1978, but had become so popular that another Morris had to be found. His trainer, Bob Martuick, found him to be a real sybarite—very lazy and only wanting to bask in the sun for hours. Today's Morris travels first class, and he earns quite a lot of money for having to work for a total of about 20 days. The first Morris became so famous that a biography was written about him. He was buried in his hometown of Loubard, Illinois.

Probably the first cat to gain international recognition through literature was Fitzy, the cat owned by Dick Whittington during the 14th century. Now the subject of pantomimes, Dick and his cat ventured to foreign lands, where Fitzy earned his master the gratitude, as well as the fortune, of a king whose land was plagued with mice. Fitzy eradicated them, and when the now-wealthy Dick returned to London, he was made the Lord Mayor. In actual fact, Richard Whittington was Lord Mayor of that capital, serving three terms. His cat is portrayed in a painting in Westminster Abbey, while a statue of Fitzy can be seen on Highgate Hill, London, where part of the story took place.

Another cat that became very famous in books was Grandville's *Puss in Boots*, who delighted 19th century children with his adventures. In more recent times, Pat Sullivan's *Felix the Cat* was extremely well known in comic strips of the 1930s. I am sure that most people know of the grinning Cheshire cat that could become invisible. He was made famous by Lewis Carroll in the tales of *Alice in Wonderland.* For nearly a century, the timeless tales of Beatrix Potter have enthralled small children, and some of her stories are based on the cat, Tabitha Twitchet.

In England, Korky the Cat delighted millions of children with his antics in a weekly comic strip, and he had his counterparts in France, Germany, and other countries. Even in Russia, there are famous story cats, such as Leopold and Matroskin. In all of these stories and caricatures, the cat is invariably seen in the role of portraying all that is good and playful in the feline. However some cats, such as the famous Warner Bros. cartoon cat Sylvester, are

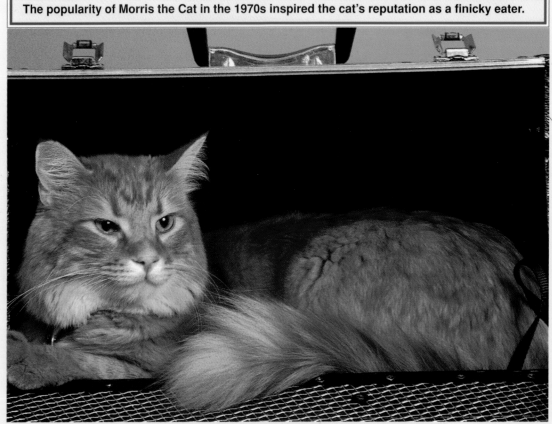

The popularity of Morris the Cat in the 1970s inspired the cat's reputation as a finicky eater.

villains, continually trying, though unsuccessfully, to eat Tweety Bird, the canary. The same is true of a similar cat, Tom, who is forever chasing Jerry, the mouse. In *Top Cat,* we see the alley cat using all of his skills in order to show his friends how to remain one step ahead of both dogs and people.

This human fascination to place the cat in a caricature setting continues to this day, and many in the western world are aware of that ever-hungry and truly delightful feline, Garfield, the creation of Jim Davis. This cat has gained almost a cult following,

and is seen in the movies, on TV, in books, in comic strips, and is produced in hundreds of cuddly toy forms. Unlike many of his predecessors, Garfield is fat, greedy, conniving, and totally selfish. Like so many real cats, he totally dominates his owner, and his only friend (other than Jon, his owner) is Odie the dog, whom Garfield regards as very inferior to a feline.

The cat has even made it big on the musical stage. The smash hit *Cats* continues to delight audiences around the world, and is based on T.S. Eliot's original book, *Old*

Possum's Book of Practical Cats, which was first published in 1939.

There are many more famous cats, and famous people who own them. But the most famous of them all are surely the cats you own, for these are all of the storybook characters rolled into one. In your cats, you can see all of the others—the good, the naughty, the greedy, and the lazy. This is why you can so easily associate with both the famous people who have owned cats, and the cats that have delighted you over the years with their antics.

Could these hungry creatures be auditioning for a pet food commercial?

Cats are sometimes known for their artistic temperaments. . .

THE CAT IN ART

Over the centuries, the cat has inspired many artists to portray felines using a wealth of different mediums, each artist perceiving the cat in a personal way. Cats are seen on frescos, canvasses, stained glass windows, and in medieval manuscripts. They appear on the tombs of the ancient Egyptians, and as illustrations in fairy tales in books, as well as a means of imparting a message in advertisements. They are represented in marble, glass, wood, stone, clay, brass, precious metals, and even papier-mache.

Cats have been depicted on old coins, and are a growing collectible on the postage stamps of many nations. In museums from New York to London, Paris and Rome, the cat is always a favorite exhibit for many people. Artists have always displayed an interest in these animals. Some concentrate on the beauty of the cat, but most attempt to define its character through the medium of the canvas.

Through the works of artists and craftsmen of long ago, we are able to piece together a mental picture of the development of the cat through the ages. The graphic representation of felines on Egyptian wall paintings, or on medieval religious woodcuts, can tell us much about the way the cat was perceived. In this chapter, we will talk not only of painters and the cats in their works, but of cats in porcelain, or metal, which is

just as fascinating. With so many paintings to select from, those discussed here represent but a sampling of many artists who have depicted the cat in its many guises. Only those showing the cat as a creature of beauty are reviewed, and they serve to illustrate the fact that many were done at a time when cats were being persecuted, thus indicating that there were many people during such times who did not support the notion of those who regarded the cat as evil.

Cats have always proved to be a considerable challenge to the artist, as evidenced by the relative lack of accurate portraits of felines. Invariably, artists have tended to try to capture the essence of the cat—or maybe they regarded it as something amusing. Very often, the cat plays a secondary role in the canvas, being almost a prop to a central figure. But there have also been a number of artists who were both cat owners and dedicated to portraying them as the sole object of the canvas.

. . .which run the gamut from mellow to *extremely* demanding.

A cat's mere presence has inspired many an artist's creation.

EGYPTIAN & ROMAN ART

The first artists to portray the cat were those of ancient Egypt. It is indeed fortunate for us that they had the habit of decorating walls and tombs with their works, otherwise we would know much less about their day-to-day lives than we do. One of the earliest known paintings is that of an idealized family life seen in a wall painting of the 18th Dynasty (1550-1070 B.C.). In it is a man (Nebamun) catching wild fowl. His wife and a cat are seen in the painting. It is highly unlikely that the cat is domestic, though many writers of cat books have interpreted it as such.

From this period forward, numerous paintings are found which clearly depict domestic cats. Others are almost certainly of tame Cheetahs, which were used as hunting aids by the Egyptians. The cat is portrayed in many Egyptian texts and paintings in the form of the goddess Bast, a cat-headed woman. The fact that all of these wall paintings depict tabby cats strongly suggests that no color mutations were known to the early Egyptians.

Unlike the Egyptians, the Romans did not worship the cat. Being very practical, they depicted it in day-to-day settings, as is shown in a mosaic from Pompeii in the first century B.C.. Here, a spotted cat has pinned a chicken to the ground. Given that it is a ceramic mosaic, it has been effected to a very high standard of accuracy. The same can be said of many Roman mosaics and frescos. With the decline of the Roman Empire, there was also a decline in the standard of art for a number of centuries.

The cat has been featured in a vast array of paintings, including Tiki art.

The cat adds the perfect finishing touch to any *chef d'oeuvre!*

THE WORKS OF SELECTED ARTISTS

It is appropriate to begin this look at the works of famous artists with Leonardo da Vinci (Italy 1452-1519). One of the most talented men the world has ever known, da Vinci was very much a cat lover. "Even the smallest creature of the cat's family is a masterpiece," he wrote. To him, the cat was a creature of great beauty, and he dedicated the painting, *Madonna with a Cat* to it. The cat is also featured in a series of sketches he did of the Holy Family. In one, a child is held by the Virgin Mary, and the child, in turn, holds a cat. There is no demonic sense in da Vinci's work, only the beauty of the feline in its many moods, from playing, to grooming, to displaying his anger—all are captured in the many sketches that have survived the passing of centuries.

Another of the early well-known artists who depicted a cat in his works was Albrecht Dürer (German, 1471-1528). In his portrayal of the *Garden of Eden*, a cat is seen at the feet of Adam and Eve. The Flemish painter Frans Floris (1516-70) also used the setting of the Garden of Eden in which to feature a cat. During the

same century, another Flemish artist, Roelandt Savery, placed the cat into one of his many landscape scenes. Here, the cat rests on the axle of a large cartwheel.

The Italian artist Lorenzo Lotto (1480-1556) in his *Annunciation*, places a

It is perhaps fitting that the master himself, Leonardo da Vinci, depicted the cat with both reverence and grandeur.

running tabby between an angel and the Virgin Mary. Often interpreted as the Devil fleeing from the angel, this seems unlikely given the fact that other artists at this time all depicted the cat as a creature of beauty and

fertility, not of an animal with demonic associations. For many artists, the cat no doubt seemed a logical choice to feature with children or females.

Pieter Bruegel the Elder (Dutch 1525-69) depicted a cat in his work, *Mary's Death*. Frans Snyders (1579-1657), a student of the renowned Rubens, continued the tradition of great Dutch painters. He was especially noted for his portrayal of cats and other animals. He graphically illustrates the cat's diverse behaviors in canvasses such as *Fish Store with a Cat*, *A Dog and a Cat*, and a *Fox and a Cat*.

Paul Rubens (Dutch, 1577-1640) also featured cats in certain works. One of these shows a large tabby sleeping near a basket, where it personifies the comforts of a home life in *Message to Mary*. David Teniers (Dutch, 1610-90), was another superb landscape painter who sometimes included the cat in his canvasses.

During the 16th century, the Italian Bernadino Luini (d. 1532), who followed the style of Leonardo da Vinci, featured a blotched tabby in his canvas, *Last Supper*. In a marquetry by Raffael da Bresica (Italy, 16th century), a blotched tabby is also depicted, which may suggest that this mutation was of Italian origin, even though it became strongly associated with England. Other Italian artists of the same period also featured this tabby pattern in their works. Staying with the Italian artists, Ulissi Aldovrandi produced a watercolor study of a cat around 1580. It suggests a tabby, but is a poor depiction of a feline.

The renowned portrait painter of French royalty, Elizabeth Vigee-Lebrun (1755-1842) was one of many famous French artists who featured cats in their work. Antoine Watteau (1684-1721), Edouard Manet (1832-83), Pierre Renoir (1841-1919) and Henri Rousseau (1844-1910) are but four of these. Renoir's style and affection for felines was ideally suited to express the sensuality of the cat. The Parisian portrait painter Jean-Babtiste Perronneau (1715-83) maintained his love of the color blue in *Girl with a Cat*, done in 1745. Here, we see a tabby of the Angora type.

The cats painted by Pablo Picasso, Max Beckmann, and Paul Klee, all of whom lived in the present century, are colorful. They were done in the impressionist or abstract style. However, they would not appeal to cat lovers who prefer paintings that represent cats in a more natural manner.

While most of the artists did their work in color, this is not so of the Swiss artist

Perhaps Reubens would have interpreted the quintessential cat in a pose such as this one.

Most cats are natural born models. This Maine Coon was once judged the Best Cat at the Cat Show in Madison Square Garden.

Only a cat could make the very act of receiving an award nothing short of an art form!

Gottfried Mind, or the Frenchman Lambert, both of whom excelled in pencil drawings. In each case, their cats are not supportive subjects, but the object of the drawings. The noted 20th century English artist Sir Edwin Landseer, though famous for his works featuring lions, did a few domestic cats. One of the most interesting is a work done in pencil of a Persian cat's head and tail. It was sketched by Landseer in 1912, when he was just 10 years old—a clear case of a child prodigy!

A Swiss artist who was able to really capture the cat in all of its moods was Alexandre Steinlen. His works, produced at the turn of the century, include both portraits of felines, as well as a whole series of illustrations that were used to promote products, from milk to tea. He was able to really express the cat's grace of movement in its many positions.

Another artist who specialized in cats was Henriette Ronner. Her paintings are quite magnificent, both for their color and the way she was able to fully capture every little movement and expression in her subjects. *Maternal Bliss*, *Four Persian Cats*, *A Cat Defending Itself Against Dogs*, and *Round The World*, are but a few of her canvasses. She was deserving of the many accolades given her, and must rank as one of the greatest feline artists of all time.

While all the artists mentioned in this chapter have been European, the cat has been represented in Near and Far Eastern paintings. Those of Turkey are interesting because from them, we are able to see the original Persian and Angora cats. Unfortunately, the cats are invariably a very minor part of the paintings, and their detail is usually rather poor.

In contrast, those of China and Japan reveal the exquisite and delicate style so characteristic of these artistic people. Many are painted onto silks. One of these, credited to Hsuan Tsung during the Ming Dynasty (1368-1644), shows a beautiful white kitten, as well as an unusually marked tabby and white. A tortie and white is also depicted in another silk by the same artist. Many 19th century silk paintings display cats of a foreign type in a range of colors and markings.

It is perhaps fitting to end this all too brief discussion of the cat in art by singling out Harrison Weir (England, 1824-1905), the organizer of the first cat show, and the man held to be the Father of the Cat Fancy. Apart from his many other abilities, he was a superb artist. His portrayals, in ink and pencil, of British cats, Persian, Siamese, and other foreign breeds, clearly show his talent to faithfully reproduce a true likeness of the breeds. Thanks to his works, we have an excellent notion of how the breeds appeared during his time.

Artists representing every medium have attempted to capture the cat's graceful and elusive qualities.

Although his "roar" may sound rather cowardly at this point in time. . .

Feline Anatomy & Senses

All felids, from the tiny black-footed cat of Africa to the awesome lions and tigers, are very similar in both their anatomy and their senses. Differences between cats are essentially related to size and cosmetics, such as their color or fur pattern. They are all highly developed and go about their predatory role in a very efficient way. The domestic cat has retained, in most varieties, all of the attributes of its wild cousins.

He may look like a gentle little ball of fur when contentedly curled up and purring on your lap, but beneath that veneer of domestication there is still a potentially savage and ruthless killer. Watch him when he spots a mouse or bird nearby, and see all of his primeval urges and capacities rise to the surface.

BASIC ANATOMY

The skeleton of the cat is basically similar in many respects to that of most other predatory mammals. It is designed to be extremely flexible. The cranium is roughly oval in shape, and the muzzle is short. This allows the cat to move its lower mandible in such a way that the enlarged dagger-

like canine teeth can be used when biting into the prey.

. . .soon this Somalie kitten's vast repertoire will sound more like that of his relative, the lion.

A cat's legs are either of medium to short length, or rather long, depending on the way in which the cat hunts its prey. Most species, including the domestic cat, have medium length of leg. The bones are relatively thick, enabling them to accommodate the good-sized muscles needed for powerful bursts of speed. Cats are essentially stalker-sprinters, which means they tire rather rapidly when at full stretch.

The longer-legged cheetah, serval, and caracal, however, display better capacity to maintain speed for greater distances.

The cat's anatomy has evolved to do things at one of two speeds—very fast or very slow. It is also designed to let the cat climb very efficiently. This is possible because of the claws, and because the paws are extremely flexible. Cats walk on their toes, a stance known as digitigrade. Such a

stance is usually associated with fleet-footed animals, but horses, which move on their nails (unguligrade), and bears, which travel on the soles of their feet (plantigrade), are also capable of traveling at a very rapid pace.

The cat's tail is relatively long in most species. Its main function is to act as a counterbalance when the cat is running and climbing. The species with the longest and

The cat's a ability to reach and climb is achieved by a highly efficient structural design of the limbs.

The cat's natural instincts remain in evidence despite centuries of domestication.

thickest tails, such as the clouded leopard, the marbled cat, and the margay, are thus the best climbers and most agile of all felids. The domestic cat can be considered about average for the cat family.

The cat is equipped with very formidable defense and attack capabilities in the form of its teeth and claws. These are a deadly combination! The claws of all species, with the exception of the cheetah, are retractable. Muscles on their lower sides keep them sheathed. When they are needed, muscles on the superior edge are retracted, while those below are relaxed. This double action pulls the claws out of their bulbous sheaths. The claws are kept razor sharp by clawing against a rough surface—which is why you should

Retractable claws allow the cat to grip and scratch, and exhibit a formidable defense mechanism.

You should always provide a scratching post for your cat, as this will keep his claws sharp without damaging your furniture.

always provide a scratching post for your cats.

When attacking its prey, the claws are used to gain a good hold on the prey while the cat finds the most appropriate place in which to sink its fangs. This will either be between the bones of the upper neck, or in the throat. The hind claws are used to rake and cut the abdomen of the prey. There are five claws on the front feet and four on the rear.

The canine teeth of a cat are highly developed, while the incisor teeth are rather small. The upper and lower molars and premolars are used to slice, rather than crush, food. The last premolar and first molars are collectively called the carnasial teeth. The cat is not able to cope with large bones,

Cats never chew a bone because their teeth were designed to slice, rather than clamp onto, food.

A cat's sense of taste is adequately developed to render his palate discriminating.

which is why it only kills animals smaller than itself. The exceptions are the big cats, which tackle prey of almost any size; but even they leave the very large bones to the likes of the hyena or hunting dogs, which can crush them.

FELINE SENSES

The cat's senses of taste, smell, hearing, and sight are excellent—even allowing for domestication.

Taste: The taste buds of a cat are positioned along the edges of theA cat's sense of taste is adequately developed to render his palate discriminating.

tongue, as well as on the tip and back. Most cats do not enjoy sweetened foods, nor those that are heavily salted. However, many cats enjoy a few licks of ice cream, which is sweetened, while wild cats will lick natural salt. This establishes the fact that they will take most things in moderation, even if they cannot be regarded as liking them in general. Although it is often stated that the cat's sense of taste is not well developed, I think this is misleading. Cats can indeed discriminate as well as any other animal, but its preferred tastes are within a defined group, namely meats.

Smell: This is a highly developed sense in cats. Indeed, so advanced is their sense of smell that when compared to that of a human that the cat has no need to taste many objects. It is able to extract all the data its brain needs about a food simply. In

Cats have much better equipped senses of hearing than humans, especially when detecting the range of higher-pitched sounds.

comparative terms, the cat's sense of smell is roughly four times better than that of a human, while a dog's is roughly seven times better than that of a cat.

Hearing: Cats have very keen hearing, especially in the high frequency range. They can hear noises we cannot, and can even hear somewhat better than a dog. This is not surprising because not only are they natural nocturnal hunters, but they also prey on small rodents that communicate in the ultra high frequency bands. The cat can tune into such sounds and pinpoint with great accuracy where they are coming from. This tuning is possible because cats, like dogs and horses, can rotate the outer ear towards a sound without having to turn their heads.

Once they are satisfied that they know which direction the sound is coming from, they then turn their heads so both ears can better focus on it, while their eyes concentrate on the approximate location in order to discern visible movement. Your cat can even hear insects beneath your floorboards, and can distinguish your footsteps from those of a stranger.

Eyesight: In terms of focusing ability, the cat

The four eyes represented here belong to Japanese Bobtail littermates, who, like all cats, have the extraordinary ability to see in complete darkness.

compares equally with a human. In relation to its face, the eyes of a cat are comparable to ours in location. Its binocular vision is in the order of 130°, while its full field of vision is about 280°. It has far superior side vision than a human, and much better binocular vision than the dog, although the dog has better lateral vision. However, altered breeds, such as the Persian, have improved binocular vision, but less lateral vision—the same being true of dog breeds such as the Pekingese and the Pug.

For a long time it was thought that cats could not distinguish between colors, seeing them only as shades of black and white. We know that they can see colors, and perhaps it is not as important to them as it is to us. This is probably why they did not respond well to color tests.

Cats have the unhuman-like ability to see in almost total darkness. No animal can see in complete darkness, but in the natural world there is always some light, albeit minimal on a cloudy night. The cat is able to utilize what light there is to maximum effect. The cat can open its pupil wider than we can, and this allows more light to enter the eye. Furthermore, this change

Black cats were especially targeted for despicable acts during the Dark Ages because they were believed to hold satanic powers.

in the size of the pupil can be made more quickly than in a human.

The cat, moving from sunlight to shadows and back to sunlight, can change the size of its pupil extremely rapidly, in fractions of a second, where we need many seconds to make these adjustments. The distance of an object from the cat will also affect the shape of the pupil, because this will change in shape in order to focus.

Your cat's eyes are not simply a means of seeing things, they also tell the cat much about the state of other cats, or things happening around them. For example, when a cat is frightened, its pupils open fully as if trying to gain as much information about what is happening—even though it may be a sunny day when the cat would normally close its pupils.

When strange cats meet, they open their pupils much more than normal so they can focus on the features of the intruder. The eyes act as aggression indicators, and the cats will attempt to stare each other down. If you develop a strong bond with your cat you may be rewarded by the fact that the cat will let you stare at him for a few seconds without upsetting it, but always blink so the stare is broken, and talk calmly to the cat so he can relate the tone of your voice as non-aggressive.

Whiskers: You might not think that whiskers are part of the senses, but they are. Have you ever been in pitch blackness and felt the presence of something even though you could not see anything? The cat's whiskers are able to sense changes in the air vibrations, and that information is conveyed back to the brain for analysis. The correct name for the whiskers is sensory vibrissae, since each hair contains sensory cells. There are similar, though softer, vibrissae in the eyebrows, the inner part of the legs, and even on the body.

The cat can rotate his whiskers in many directions according to his needs. When he is about to jump, he will use the whiskers to gain information about wind speed and direction. Likewise, the whiskers can impart information in the dark in respect to the distance of

In terms of sensory reception and interpretation, a cat's whiskers are nothing short of a marvel of basic anatomy.

potential prey. They also enable the cat to sense branches or other objects near to its face, without the cat needing to change its eye focus. The many roles of whiskers indicate that breeds such as the rexes, which have reduced, fragile, or no whiskers, are clearly at a disadvantage to the breeds with normal vibrissae.

Memory & Intelligence: All of a cat's senses culminate in passing messages back to the brain for analysis. Each new impulse or sensation is recorded as being either positive, negative, or neutral. This imprinting is not done apart from information from other senses. For example, when a cat travels any distance, it not only records objects along the route, but also all the different smells and sounds. Each of these is used to determine the return path—so it can return easily even at night and even though some objects may not be as discernible as they were in the day.

If your cat is being naughty, and you chastize him at the same moment, he will associate your annoyance with the act. Repeated enough times, the cat generally refrains from the act. This act and reaction to it is the basis of all animal training. It establishes that cats have an excellent memory and a high degree of intelligence.

Cats are unlikely to ever compare with dogs in what they can be taught to do. There are two basic reasons for this: One is that cats are not especially social creatures in their wild state. They have no predisposition to work within a cooperative framework to achieve an objective (such as catching prey). They will accept mild discipline and then run off, exactly as they would in the wild. In other words, the cat will respond to status discipline, but not to discipline that is of a socially important nature for the survival of the pack. Of all the cats, the lion is the most easily trained, and it is also the most highly social in the wild state. It lives in prides where cooperation is vital, especially when a hunt is on.

The second factor is that cats have never been selectively bred based on an ability to modify an existing trait.

In the home of the true cat lover, it is more than likely that the cat has trained the owner than the other way around! He is intelligent enough to communicate to us when he wants to be fed; when he wants us to open the door to let him out or in; when he wants to be fussed over, and when he doesn't. He will talk to us constantly, but we are not always intuitive enough to understand what he is saying.

While the cat is known to have superior intelligence, reports of its ability to read are greatly exaggerated!

Paying careful attention to our pets will allow us to become more attuned to the language of cats, and their unique means of communication.

Cat Language

The cat has an extensive range of vocal sounds that, together with various body movements, make up its language. Over the years, a number of people have attempted to classify the various sounds cats make into a sort of feline alphabet, but such attempts have always met with failure. While we cannot hope to interpret all of the sounds a cat makes, we can draw reasonable conclusions about some of them.

Your cat will actually impart more information to you with its body than it will with its sounds. Some cats are very quiet and hardly use their voices, while others have so much to say that sometimes they can become pests. We will consider both the obvious and the not-so-obvious sounds and movements that can be useful in understanding what a cat is trying to communicate to us. Bear in mind that each cat is an individual, and is able to develop a language that is somewhat unique. This happens because he will respond in a certain way to certain actions by his owner. Furthermore, a domestic cat may retain sounds used as a kitten well into adulthood.

Clearly, if you devote time to your pet, you will come to develop an understanding of his sounds and movements much better than the owner who pays little attention to his feline companion. A number of sounds and body movements, heard and seen,

are not unique to the cat. Many other animals may have developed a very similar language because it has been found to be effective and this, after all, is what communication is all about.

The urgency and pitch of a cat's meow signals the severity of the current situation.

the hiss from the moment their eyes open. The hiss is a purely defensive sound but is not used solely on aggressors; an adult cat will hiss at a strange kitten, which means, "Keep away from me."

THE HISS

When a cat finds himself in a defensive situation, he will hiss, leaving no mistake about his state of mind or his intentions. This sound is coupled with a very obvious body posture. The cat will raise the hairs on his back and neck so as to look bigger than he really is. He will pin his ears back and will more often than not, arch his back or crouch low to the ground. He will dilate his pupils and try to menace the aggressor with his fixed stare. The youngest of kittens develop

In this case, the adult cat does not need to display all of the body movements that indicate anger, rather he will simply glare at the youngster, perhaps placing his ears back and hissing loudly. In this instance, the hiss is used as a form of discipline.

Some birds, such as geese, will use the hiss as a warning sound, as will skunks, snakes, and lizards. These animals also puff out their feathers, their fur, or their facial skin, as the case may be. Whether or not animals have developed this sound

and behavior over thousands of years is impossible to say. However, for one species of animal to copy another, or to look like another that is known to be dangerous, is quite common in the animal world.

THE GROWL

The growl is a sound that is largely restricted to the order *Carnivora*, so it is heard in cats, dogs, bears, and hyenas, for example. Once again, it is usually a defensive sound, but it can also be used as a warning that if a threat is not removed, the growler is prepared to follow through with an attack. It may also be used as an aggressive sound in order to try to frighten an adversary or a prey animal. When used in this situation, the objective is to get the prey species to stop its defensive posture and run. Cats, like many carnivores, prefer to attack animals that are moving rather than those who are standing their ground.

When a cat is being approached by a tougher cat, he will first crouch down and hiss. If the aggressor continues a forward advance, the cat will growl, which will change quite suddenly in its pitch, from low to high. It is the final defensive warning, and it may cause the aggressor to stop in his tracks if he is at all unsure of himself. The growl will then be followed by another warning hiss.

THE MEOW

Of all the cat's sounds, the meow is possibly the most variable in its tone, length, volume, and meaning. It is the one cat sound that has been modified as a result of domestication. In the wild, the meow is essentially a sound used between a mother and her kittens. The mother cat uses it in varying tones to call her babies to her, and they use it as a plea for attention or food or as a greeting. As a wild kitten matures, he has little need of such gentle language. But in the domestic environment, where he does not normally go out and catch his own food, he must find a way to communicate his needs to its owner. He obviously cannot use growls, hisses, and similar attack/defense language, so he retains his kitten language, which he develops according to the home.

The adult meow can vary from the very soft plea of a small to medium cat, to the semi-howl of a large tomcat. It may be a short sound or one that is drawn out—each cat develops his own range of meows. There will be one used as thanks when you open the door for him and another that is used when the cat has finally persuaded you to go and open the pantry door to get him some food. There is yet another meow that is used when your cat is clearly trying to tell you something but you are not responding. The bottom line of the meow is that it is a request for attention, whether the cat wants to be let out, in, given food, fussed over, or even to tell you that it's time to go to bed.

Often, the meow will be accompanied by some kind of body language. In other animals, such as dogs, ferrets, horses, or birds, the equivalent of the meow will be a whimper, a soft whinny, a sort of clucking, or any of a number of sounds that are soft and convey beseechment. In social species, these sounds will often be carried into adulthood—even within a wild species.

THE PURR

A purr can best be described in human body language as a "smile." The cat uses the purr to assure its kittens that all is well. It uses it to display non-aggression to his owner, as well as to indicate self-satisfaction. The purr of some cats is very loud, while with others it can hardly be heard at all. This is not dependent on

It is believed that domesticated cats developed selective meows to vocally communicate with humans.

the cat's size. Based on my own experiences over the years, I would say that the louder the purr, the more outgoing the nature of the cat. It is usually a lively feline that you would describe as a kitten-cat, and that has a good loud purr even when it is quite old.

THE SCREECH

No one could mistake the screech of a cat—it is clearly a sound of fear or pain. Cats use it seconds before they go into combat, at the moment of pain, and also during mating (in the case of the female). As the male withdraws his penis, the female will screech out and often try to attack the male at the moment of this action.

TWITTERING

When a cat sees a bird through the window, he will often make a sort of twittering noise. One theory is that this sound may be used by adults who are teaching their kittens to hunt. It is a kind of "stay still" command. However, there are two other possibilities; It may be a sound that indicates frustration because the cat knows he cannot pursue his prey through the glass, or whatever object prevents it from reaching the bird. Alternatively, it may be a sound that is still in its evolutionary development stage—a non-cat-like sound that is related to hunting strategy.

BODY LANGUAGE

All animals, including humans, have a repertoire of body language that can be used in association with vocal sounds or on its own. Most are inherent to the species, but others are acquired. The arched back and raised fur are obvious signs of a cat that is in a defensive posture, but the ears and tail are also used to convey information about the mood of the moment. When the ears are pinned back, this is a sign that the cat is angry, and is either about to defend himself or attack. This posture protects the ears once combat becomes a reality. It is a common form of body language that has the same meaning in many creatures.

Normal ear carriage in a cat is erect, and the ears are constantly being moved sideways, one at a time when the cat is picking up sounds. If the cat starts to twitch his ears it usually indicates he is becoming annoyed. The tail is perhaps the best visual indicator of a cat's attitude at the moment.

When carried in an erect position, the cat is quite content with himself and is confident of the world around it. If the cat moves with his tail carried low, he tends to be of a somewhat nervous disposition. Carried with a downward sweep, but with the last quarter curled upward, is a very typical carriage in contented felines.

When a cat approaches you with his tail held straight up, this is a greeting sign. In the wild, this position allows friends to sniff its rear end. This may not seem very dignified to us, but it is a very common form of greeting in animals—ranging from cats and dogs, to bears, and even apes. There is also an element of subordination in this act.

Tomcats often follow this technique by moving their tail in a sort of quick shiver, while swinging their rear end towards your leg. The shiver often, although not always, indicates that the cat is about to spray marker urine. This is not usually seen with neutered males, which will simply swing their rear quarters into your leg.

An alternative to this behavior is that the cat will rub its chin against you. This is another form of scent marking that you will find both sexes do quite a lot of— and a male will do especially if a strange tom has been in the vicinity. When your cat rubs against you with its head, he is transferring his scent onto you as a personal gesture that you are part of his community or family.

When the tail is twitched from side to side in a slow manner, this indicates that the cat is not happy about something. He is not angry, just perturbed. You may be stroking it when it doesn't want to be stroked, so it is trying to tell you to please stop. When the tail is twitched with deliberate side-to-side movements, and the pace of the twitch increases, the cat is getting very angry and may follow this with some form of aggression. If you have owned only dogs before, you will note that with cats, tail wagging represents just the opposite.

Another difference between dogs and cats is that a dog will roll over to indicate submission. He will greatly enjoy having his chest rubbed, which he finds extremely soothing. The opposite is the case in most, although not all, cats. Rolling

over to them is an invitation to play—not a submissive act. Only those cats who are really friendly will allow you to stroke their chest while they are on their back or side. Most will instinctively use their claws to grab hold of your hand or arm. They may then bite and rake with their rear claws—as they did when fighting or playing as kittens. Cats that allow you to rub their chests are granting you a special favor, and some do seem to enjoy this if it is done gently.

Of all the body language that a cat learns, probably the most frequently used is the cat's tapping you with its paws when he wants you to do something. Invariably, this is to tell you that it wants some food, but many cats also do this when they want to be fussed over. Cats may learn this behavior themselves, or they may copy it from other cats in the household.

Acquired language with cats and other kinds of household pets is the result of chance and enforcement. Take paw tapping for example. Your cat may just happen to tap you with its paw, and you may react in one of many ways. You may regard it as cute and stroke your cat. You might give the cat some food. The cat may not immediately relate the act with the other, but if this happens a second and third time, your cat is clever enough to link the two actions. Thereafter, each time the cat paws you and receives food or other attention, this reinforces the act. The tapping may then widen in scope so that the cat uses this technique to gain your attention, not just for food, but for any end result the cat finds benefiicial. All animal training is based on this technique of cause and effect, which is known as positive and negative stimuli.

You will find that if you take the time to study your cats, each will have his own special way of communicating with you. A cat will adapt his natural language to meet his needs with you as an individual. He cannot understand the definition of your words, but he can understand their tone, and he is able to read your body language. It is not a one-way street, but rather a case of both of you trying your best to establish a common language.

Paw-tapping acts as a real attention-getter in the diverse language of cats.

The Nine Lives of a Cat

I am not sure how old the saying is that a cat has nine lives, nor indeed why this number was selected. But the meaning of the myth is clear enough. There is ample evidence to show that cats are indeed remarkable for being able to survive situations that would surely kill most other animals.

During the blacker period of cats' past (the 15th century), many cats were thrown from church belfries because it was believed they had demonic powers. When you consider that uneducated peasants saw some of these cats not only survive the fall, but get up and run away, it is not difficult to understand that such people thought the cat had died on impact, and had been given another life by the Devil. Such a feat is amazing, but hardly compares with the fact that cats have fallen from 32-story skyscrapers and walked away with only minor injuries!

Cats have survived extended periods of confinement with no food or water, and have even survived sunken shipwrecks, so the myth of nine lives would certainly seem to be applicable to this species. However, there is nothing mythical about these happenings, nor of a cat's perceived extrasensory perception that people through the ages have credited the cat with owning. Most things in life can be explained in a rational manner, the escapades of the cat being no exception. However, the full explanation of certain feline abilities, such as orientation, are still not fully understood, and no doubt will be in the future.

FALLING

That cats can survive from falling many feet is evident from the number of felines manage to fall out of windows in New York, and other metropolitan areas. In one year alone, some 132 cats fell from windows ranging from the second to thirty-second floors of apartments. Of these, 104 survived relatively unhurt, 11 died from chest injuries or shock, and the remaining 17 were destroyed because their owners could not afford veterinary treatment.

Surprisingly, a cat may suffer a greater injury to himself when it falls from a low height after dozing, or being poorly handled, than if it fell from a much greater height. For example, one owner's cat was always going to sleep on—then falling off—the TV. Such a fall could easily result in a sprained or broken limb. A cat falling from its owner's arms may damage itself if it should flip early in the fall.

The explanation of these two situations may be compared to a man with a parachute jumping from a

The legendary "Nine Lives of a Cat" is derived from his uncanny ability to survive adversity.

plane. If there is not enough distance for the parachute to open, he will probably die—from a greater height the chute would open and he would live. The cat is the same. It needs time in order to spin its body towards the earth, then prepare itself for the impact. Should anything interrupt the fall, such as a tree branch, or a window ledge, the cat may not have enough height left in which to realign its body.

The mechanics of the falling process involve, in particular, the eyes, the inner ear, and the tail. If a cat is defective in any of these, then its chances of surviving a fall reduce accordingly. Therefore, kittens whose eyes have not opened are unable to correct a fall, while short-tailed breeds are not as expert as normal-tailed cats.

When the cat initially falls, the first thing that happens is that the eyes, together with a complicated organ in the ear, convey to the brain that they are not in a proper relationship to the ground.

The cat then turns his head downwards, at the same time stretching out his forelimbs, and begins to rotate its very flexible body. The tail is a crucial counter balance in this movement. It first swings, to aid the directional fall, then swings the opposite way in order to arrest the roll.

Now the cat is facing the earth and prepares for the landing. His back arches and the forelimbs stretch down. The back arches even more and the hind limbs are nearly straightened. The tail is now

This fearless feline appears to be defying gravity.

nearly straight out, helping to slow down the fall while maintaining the body's correct position. The fact that the bones of the limbs and backbone of a cat are less rigidly locked together than those of humans means the intervertebral discs can cushion the impact far better. Even so, it is a masterful display of body and brain coordination that make gymnasts look very ordinary by comparison.

AMAZING ESCAPES

As testimony to the nine lives of a cat is Jacob, a ship's cat. In 1963 the Tioba, a Dutch vessel, was traveling in inclement weather conditions in a river. The ship capsized and sank very rapidly, and the crew hardly had time to escape. Eight days later, cranes brought the vessel to the surface and the crew sought their belongings from the ship. When the captain opened his cabin door, he was staggered to see Jacob, soaked, cold, and mewing dolefully for some food! He had been saved by a pocket of air in the cabin.

Then there was the cat, Mercedes, who was accidentally entombed in a crate with machinery bound from Liverpool, England, to Nigeria, Africa—a journey of many weeks. When the crate was opened, the cat was discovered—he had survived by licking grease from the machine! The cat is able to conserve water by regulating the output based on what the input. If this is low, the cat will not urinate. This physiological fact has saved many a cat.

During the Blitz in England, many cats survived the horrendous bombings when entire housing blocks came down in fire and rubble. There are many stories of cats that somehow lived through these and crawled out weeks later, weak, cut, and bruised, but none the worse for their ordeal after treatment and a few hearty meals. Thus, the cat's ability to crouch and hide in the smallest of spaces, combined with a generous helping of good luck, is the basis of its so-called nine lives.

EXTRASENSORY PERCEPTION

There are many instances where cat owners through the ages have thought that their cats displayed extrasensory perception because they seemed able to foretell disasters. For example, cats would seek out high places in the home just before floods, or they would abandon their home just before an earthquake. These things are not difficult to understand these days because we know the cat has extremely acute senses. They can detect changes in the humidity long before we can, and they can sense the faintest tremors in the earth. They can also pick up high frequency sounds which may result in their knowing shortly before we do that a building is stressed and may collapse. Most of the cat's extrasensory powers can be explained in a scientific manner.

One aspect of a cat's ability does, however, pose a real dilemma. This is in relation to its proven ability to travel vast distances to specific locations that it has never been before. Consider the case of Sugar, a California cat, who was given to friends by his owners because they were to relocate some 1500 miles away. Two weeks after the owners left, they were advised by Sugar's new owner that the cat had disappeared.

Fourteen months later, the previous owner was working in her garden when Sugar appeared in front of her. The owner was beside herself in amazement, and friends would not accept that it was the same cat. However, an owner knows her own cat; he had the same shin bone deformity that had been present as a kitten. As incredible as such a journey may seem, it is only one of many authenticated instances of such a feat. How is it possible, and can it be explained in a rational way? The answer has to be that there is no definite explanation.

Every year, thousands of cats are lost, and never find their way home—even across relatively short distances. This fact would seem to make nonsense of the long distance cats, but in reality, it does not. It simply means that some cats, and some owners, rare though they may be, possess something that enables each to communicate with the other when no other rational explanation is possible. Such cats are using a sense that has not yet been identified. When it has, it will no longer be considered extrasensory, and another apparently magical ability in the cat will be appreciated.

Suggested Reading

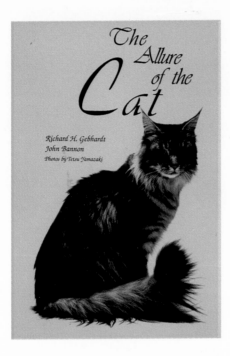

TS-173
The Allure of the Cat

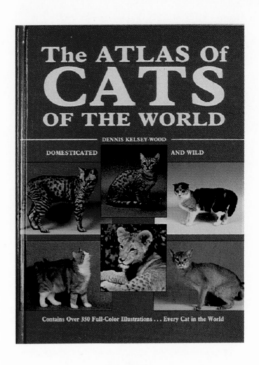

TS-127
The Atlas of Cats of the World

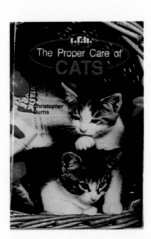

TW-103
The Proper Care of Cats

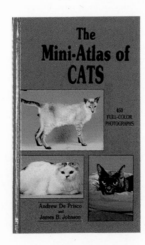

TS-152
The Mini-Atlas of Cats

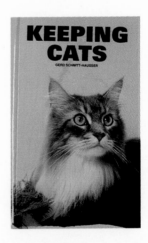

TS-219
Keeping Cats